Backyard Boo[ks]

Are you a Grasshopper?

KINGFISHER

LONDON & NEW YORK

Copyright © Kingfisher 2002
Text copyright © Judy Allen 2002

Published in the United States by Kingfisher,
175 Fifth Avenue, New York, NY 10010
Kingfisher is an imprint of Macmillan Children's Books, London.
All rights reserved.

Distributed in the U.S. and Canada by Macmillan,
175 Fifth Avenue, New York, NY 10010

Library of Congress Cataloging-in-Publication Data
Allen, Judy.
Are you a grasshopper?/by Judy Allen; illustrated by Tudor Humphries.—1st ed.
p. cm.—(Backyard books)
1. Grasshoppers—Juvenile literature. [1. Grasshoppers.] I. Humphries, Tudor, ill. II. Title.
QL508. A2 A64 2001
595.7'26—dc21

ISBN 978-0-7534-5806-8

Kingfisher books are available for special promotions and premiums. For details contact:
Special Markets Department, Macmillan, 175 Fifth Avenue, New York, NY 10010.

For more information, please visit www.kingfisherbooks.com

Printed in China
11
11TR/0614/WKT/DIG(MA)/128MA

Backyard Books

Are You a Grasshopper?

Judy Allen and Tudor Humphries

KINGFISHER
NEW YORK

Are you a grasshopper?

If you are, your mother looks like this.

Your father looks much the same.

Your mother laid her eggs
at the end of the summer.
She laid them deep in the grass,
just under the ground,
and covered them in frothy stuff.
The froth hardened into a pod
to keep the eggs safe.

You and your brothers
and sisters slept in
your eggs all winter—
but now it's spring.

Time to hatch.

Push all together
to get out of the pod.

You look a little like
a tiny worm, but
that's only because
you're wrapped in a
worm-shaped covering.

So unwrap yourself.

You're still tiny, and you don't have
any wings, but now you look
like a grasshopper.

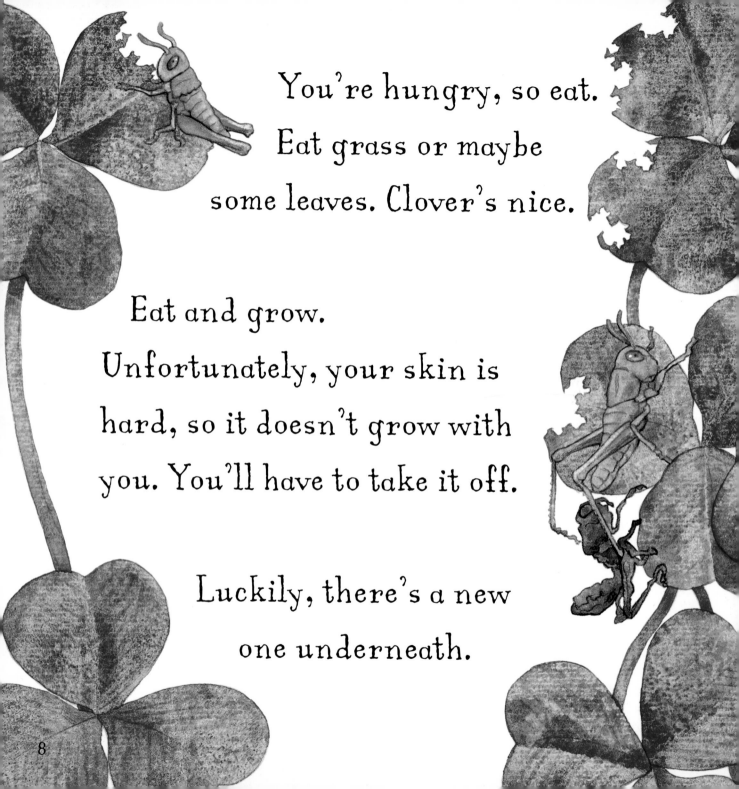

You're hungry, so eat.
Eat grass or maybe
some leaves. Clover's nice.

Eat and grow.
Unfortunately, your skin is
hard, so it doesn't grow with
you. You'll have to take it off.

Luckily, there's a new
one underneath.

Eat and grow and change your skin again. Now you have wing buds on your back.

Change your skin again.

Now you have small, stubby wings.

9

Eat and grow and change
your skin at least four times.

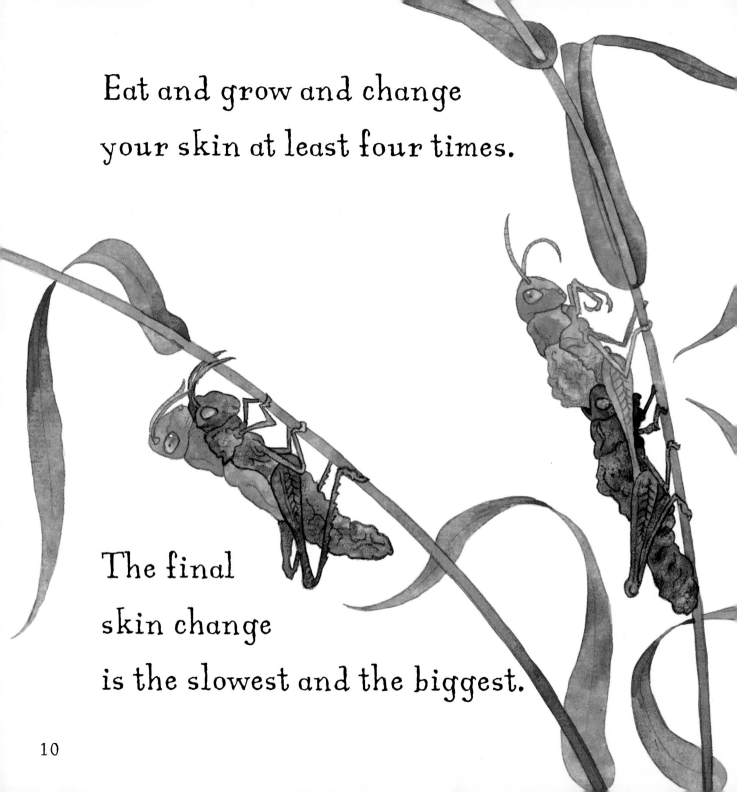

The final
skin change
is the slowest and the biggest.

Struggle out of your old
skin and hang from
a grass stem

while your wings
grow to full size.

At last
you are a fully grown grasshopper.

You're bigger and stronger than before.
You have six legs, two pairs of wings,
two large eyes, and two short feelers.

You have tiny ear holes on the sides
of your body, above your
back pair of legs.

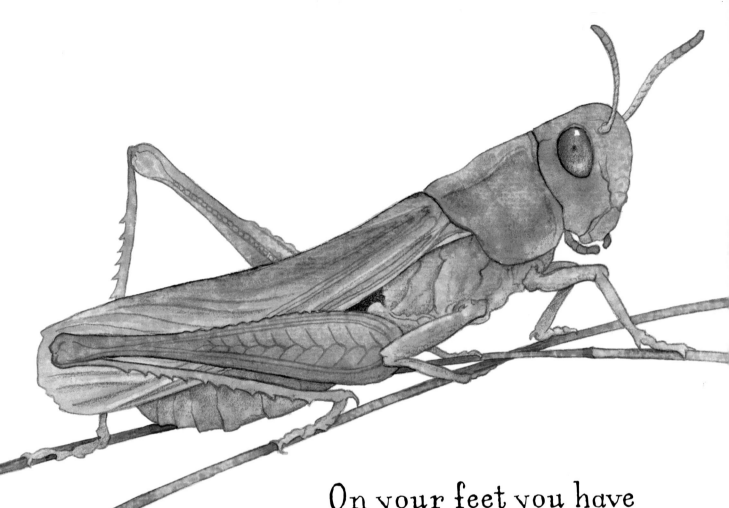

On your feet you have
suction pads, so you can cling to stems.
Beside your mouth you have palpi, like
tiny fingers, to help push in your food.

This is a bush cricket.

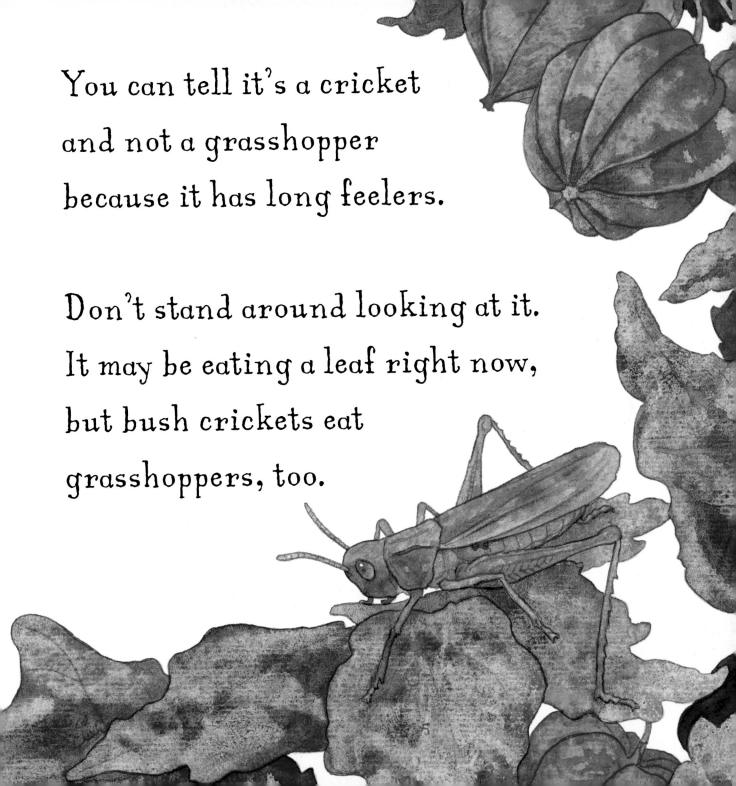

You can tell it's a cricket
and not a grasshopper
because it has long feelers.

Don't stand around looking at it.
It may be eating a leaf right now,
but bush crickets eat
grasshoppers, too.

Don't get caught
in a spiderweb.
Spiders eat grasshoppers.

Don't get too close
to a frog or a toad.
Frogs and toads
eat grasshoppers.

Watch out for birds.

Some birds eat grasshoppers too.

It's a dangerous world out there in the grass.

Always be ready
to escape from danger.

You could fly—
except you're
not very good at flying.

You could hide.

You're very difficult
to see if you creep
down among
the grass stems.

Or you could hop.
After all, you ARE
a grasshopper.

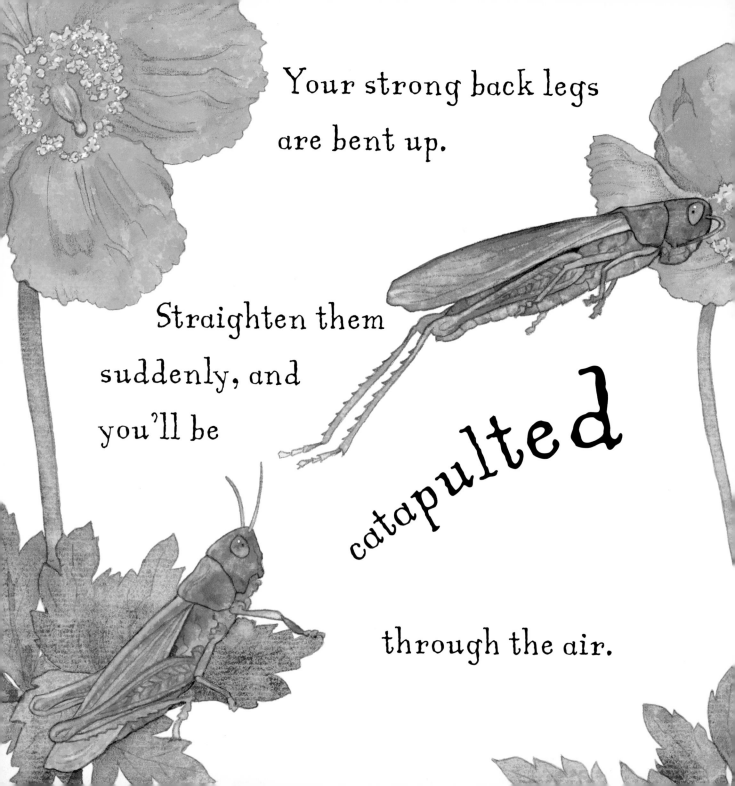

Your strong back legs are bent up.

Straighten them suddenly, and you'll be

catapulted

through the air.

You can jump amazingly
high and travel an
amazingly long way.

You're very light,
and your skin is like a
suit of armor. You won't
hurt yourself when you land.

You have a row of tiny pegs on the inside of each leg. Pedal your legs up and down fast. The pegs rub against your wings and make a ticking, chirping noise.

Keep going for about twenty seconds.

Have a break.

Then start again.

If you are a male
grasshopper, chirp
loudly to attract a mate.

If you are a female
grasshopper, you can
chirp back if you want to.

The important thing
is to mate and lay eggs
for next year.

23

However, if your mother and father
look like this

or this

or this

you are not a grasshopper.

You are...

...a human child.

You don't have wings.

You don't have feelers.

You don't have ears in
the sides of your body.

You probably
can't jump
amazingly high.

Don't worry, you can do many things
a grasshopper can't do.

Best of all, you can make music
without pedaling your legs
up and down.

Did You Know...

...the grasshoppers in this book are common green grasshoppers, but there are more than 7,000 different kinds of grasshoppers. Also, they are closely related to crickets, stick insects, cockroaches, and earwigs.

...a grasshopper can jump 20 times the length of its own body.

...the locust is
a large, tropical
grasshopper that is
very good at flying.
A swarm of locusts can eat a
whole field of crops in one night.

...most grasshoppers die at the
end of the summer, after they've
laid their eggs.